OUR CHURCH

a guide
for young people

by

H. W. Dobson

*Author of Church Teaching for the
Junior Child Books I–IV, In Excelsis,
The Christian Year.*

Illustrated by T. R. Williams

1962
CHURCH INFORMATION OFFICE
Church House Westminster SW1

This book has been published by the
Church Information Office for the
Children's Council—one of the Councils of the
Church of England Board of Education

© H. W. Dobson, 1962

PRINTED IN GREAT BRITAIN AT
THE VILLAFIELD PRESS, BISHOPBRIGGS, GLASGOW

TO OUR READERS

You can start this book at any time you like, but the last nine chapters should be read at the time when the Seasons they are about come round.

The 'Things to do' are important. Do not leave them out. Try and do as many as you can—the harder ones as well as the easier ones.

For this you will need:

A LARGE SCRAPBOOK for pictures and photographs which you will be collecting from newspapers and magazines;

A NOTE BOOK for drawing and writing;

A PRAYER BOOK, A HYMN BOOK and A BIBLE. It will be a help to have the *New English Bible* or *The New Testament in modern English* (J. B. Phillips) as well as the Authorised Version.

If you go to see any fresh churches when you are away or on holiday, do not forget to take your camera. You will be sure to get some good pictures to put in your scrapbook along with other photographs you may collect.

If you have enjoyed using this book, perhaps you can persuade someone to give you for your birthday a book called *What to See in a Country Church*, by L. E. Jones. It is published by Phoenix House Ltd.

CONTENTS

I *THE PARISH CHURCH*

For hundreds of years our country has been divided up into parishes, and in one of these is your home. Do you know the name of the parish in which you live?

Every parish has its own parish church. Do you know the name of yours? Perhaps it is called after one of the apostles—St Peter, St Andrew or St John—or after some Christian saint of olden times. You yourself bear a name which is your very own—your Christian name; and churches, like people, have their own special names too.

I expect you know where your parish or mission church is, what it looks like from the outside and how it is different from the churches in the pictures in this chapter. No two parish churches are exactly alike.

Every parish has its own parish priest, called rector, vicar, or priest-in-charge. He takes the services in church and visits people in their homes. Sometimes in a very large parish he has a curate to help him.

Wherever we go in our country there will be a parish, a parish church and a parish priest, so we need never miss joining in the Sunday services when we are away from home or on holiday.

Before exploring the inside of our parish church, let us look at it from the outside and learn the names of the different parts. The picture on the previous page will help us.

First, notice the *chancel*. Inside this part of the church we shall find the altar or holy table. The prayer desk of the parish priest is generally there too and so are the stalls for the choir. The chancel lies at the east end of the church, so it is a good 'direction-finder' whenever you are out cycling or hiking in strange country.

Then there is the *nave*, where most of the people sit when they come to church. Perhaps that is where you sit.

The *vestry* is the place in which the parish priest, and sometimes the choir, get ready for the services. Their robes and vestments are kept there and so are the communion vessels. In the vestry is a large safe where the church registers are kept; among them are the baptism registers in which are written the names of those who have been made members of God's great family. Your name is in the register of the church in which you were baptized.

Most churches have either a *tower* or a *spire* where the church bells hang. As church towers and spires generally stand high above the buildings round about, they help us to pick out and find the parish church more easily. They also point upwards like a finger to remind us of God.

Do you know why our fore-fathers built so many lovely parish churches and why people today are still building them in new towns and on housing estates? It is because those who belong to the family of God, his holy Catholic

CLAYPOLE CHURCH,
LINCOLNSHIRE

Church, need a place where they can meet together for worship—especially on Sunday, the Lord's day. They remember that the Lord Jesus said, 'Where two or three are gathered together in my name, there am I in the midst of them.'

You belong to that family; you became a member of it when you were baptized; you too have your own special place—with the Lord's people, in the Lord's house, on the Lord's day.

EVERCREECH, SOMERSET

Things to do

1. Find a picture of your own parish church and paste it in your scrapbook. Write underneath its full name and the name of your parish or district. Be sure you know which is the chancel, nave, tower and vestry. If you cannot find a picture try to draw one.
2. Write in your notebook (1) the name of your rector, vicar, or priest-in-charge; (2) the names and times of the services held on Sundays, putting a star against the one which you attend.
3. Make up a prayer asking for God's blessing on your parish church and parish and then use it yourself.

Harder things to do

1. Find out all you can about your parish church—its size, its age, etc., and about your parish—its boundaries, the number of people who live in it, etc.
2. In this chapter we have used the word 'church' to mean a building—except in one place. Can you find that place and say what the other meaning is? When you have talked about it to your parents or teachers, write down that other meaning in your own words in your notebook.
3. Find in your Bible, Acts, chapter 12, verses 1–12, and read the story. It tells how God answered the prayers of Christians many years ago when they met together for worship. What things do you think God's family should ask for when they meet together for worship today?

2 The story of AN ANCIENT CHURCH

Many of our parish churches are hundreds of years old.
Here is a story about one of them.

Long ago, when England was still divided into separate
kingdoms, the Christian King Oswy reigned in Northumbria. When he was about to go
into battle against a neighbouring
king who was a heathen, he vowed
a vow to God: 'If I am victorious
in battle', he said 'I will give my
daughter, Elfleda, to the service of
God'.

Oswy's prayer was answered
and he won a great victory; so
Elfleda, who was still a little girl,
was taken to learn to serve God in
the abbey or monastery of Heruteu
—a place today called Hartlepool.
It is a seaside town in the County
of Durham, lying a few miles
north of the River Tees.

No doubt at first Elfleda felt
lonely in her strange surroundings,
but she need not have done, for in
those days the good Saint Hilda
ruled the abbey at Hartlepool. She
was very kind and was loved by all,
so that they called her 'Mother'.

Elfleda soon felt quite at home in the monastery with Mother Hilda and the monks and nuns. They spent much of their time worshipping God in the monastery church, studying the Bible and teaching others about the Lord Jesus. Elfleda loved her life in the monastery, and when she grew up she went with Hilda to Whitby. There Elfleda herself became the abbess after Hilda died.

But unhappy times were in store for Hartlepool; fierce Danish invaders swooped down upon it from their ships and burned down the monastery; not a stone was left standing!

For many years there was no church, no house of God in Hartlepool. Then William the Conqueror gave lands there to Robert de Brus (or Bruce). He was one of those who had come over with William from Normandy when he invaded England in 1066. Robert de Brus and his family were Christians, and when Robert went to take over his new possessions he heard the sad story of Saint Hilda's famous monastery church and how the cruel Viking raiders had destroyed it.

When Robert told his family about this they said, '*We* must build them a *new* church.'

So Robert went to the people of Hartlepool and said, 'I and my family will build you a new church, and we will call it after the blessed Saint Hilda.'

That is how the church which you can see in the picture on the next page came to be built. We do not know exactly when they started to build it, but the church as we know it now was finished about 1260, and William de Brus, one of Robert's descendants, had much to do with finishing it. So once more the people of

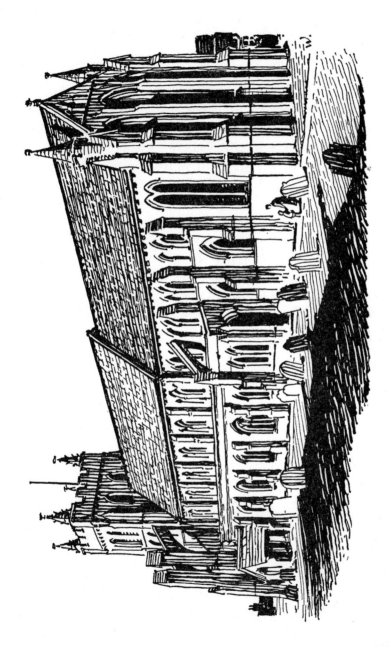

Hartlepool had a lovely building in which they could meet together to worship God.

The last of the Brus family to be Lord of Hartlepool and, we may believe, to have worshipped in St Hilda's church, was the most famous of them all. Our history books know him as Robert the Bruce. Perhaps you remember how one day when Robert was hiding in a cave from his enemies, a spider saved his life; for after he climbed inside, it spun its web over the entrance, making his pursuers think there was no one there!

You may remember too how Robert the Bruce defeated the English king, Edward the Second, at the battle of Bannockburn and became King of Scotland. It is said that before the battle Robert and all his soldiers knelt on the battlefield to receive the Holy Communion. The English king and his army were not far away and they could see them.

'Yonder folk kneel', the English king shouted, 'they ask for mercy.'

'True', said an English knight who was standing by, 'they ask for mercy, but not from you. They cry to God for help.'

Perhaps Robert the Bruce remembered the lovely church of St Hilda where, with the people of Hartlepool, he and his family had learned to worship God and seek his help.

For more than seven hundred years services have been held in St Hilda's, Hartlepool, as in many another ancient church in our land. Throughout the centuries people have gone there week by week to worship God and to seek his help, and they do so still.

Things to do

1. Find and mark Hartlepool and Whitby on the map.
2. There are some exciting scenes for you to draw in this story. Make a strip cartoon of scenes in the life of *either* Elfleda *or* Robert the Bruce.
3. Whitby is only one of many famous abbeys and monasteries in England. Is there a monastery, or the ruins of one, near your home? If so, find out all you can about it, and try to visit it.

Harder things to do

1. Every day in the services of the monastery Elfleda and Hilda joined in saying or singing the psalms. Find Psalms 121 and 134 in your Prayer Book, and, if you can, write in one sentence what each of them is about.
2. Find in your Bible and read these passages which remind us of St Hilda:

    St Mark, chapter 10, verses 43 and 44; Philippians, chapter 4, verse 8; Colossians, chapter 3, verses 16 and 17.
3. Find the Collect for the 22nd Sunday after Trinity, make sure you understand it, then use it as a prayer for St Hilda's, Hartlepool, and all parish churches.

3 *The story of* *A MODERN CHURCH*

Standing on a lorry, facing an old, unwanted church in London, an army officer turned priest commanded in a loud voice, 'In the name of Jesus Christ be thou removed to Biggin Hill.' And it was!

The story began when Biggin Hill was still a small village in Kent, with only a tiny temporary church made of red corrugated iron. Then the Royal Air Force set up a base on Biggin Hill and soon hundreds more people came to live there. The tiny church was no longer big enough, and besides, it was nearly worn out. Though there was only a little money in hand for a new church something just had to be done.

In 1951 a new vicar came to Biggan Hill. His name was Vivian Symons. He thought much about the new church that the people needed. 'It is true that we cannot afford a new church', he said to himself, 'but if we could find an old one somewhere, that nobody wants, we might move it here. It need not cost a great deal of money if we do the work ourselves.'

So Mr Symons and some of the people of Biggin Hill looked round for a closed, unwanted church, and found one at Peckham in London, nineteen miles away. They got permission to take it down and build it again in their own parish.

In August 1952 the vicar of Biggin Hill drove down the Old Kent Road to Peckham in a battered Morris

lorry, which a London builder had given him. He got safely to Peckham and started to take down the old church. That was how the work on 'The Moving Church' began. Sometimes Mr Symons had help from the congregation of Biggin Hill; sometimes he worked on his own. You can see him in the picture with a pick in his hand. Hundreds upon hundreds of loads of bricks, stone and wood were taken away in the old lorry to Biggin Hill.

Many Londoners were surprised to see a vicar doing a grimy, dusty job like this! One day when Mr Symons was in a café near by, having a cup of tea, a woman nudged her companion and said 'Cor! Now I've seen everything.'

It took three years and four months to move the church. Biggin Hill now had 125,000 bricks, all cleaned and stacked, mostly by the ladies of the church; 200 tons of stonework and all the roof timbers from the old church, not to mention countless tiles taken from the roof.

Lots of people came to know about 'The Moving Church' through the newspapers and TV. Many sent gifts of money, and in 1958 a local firm of builders began to build the new church of St Mark, Biggin Hill. You can see what it looks like from the picture on the next page. The number of bricks from the old church were within but a few hundred of the number wanted for the new; there was just enough of the old stonework, and all the old timbers fitted together again perfectly to make the roof for the new building.

Many people in Biggin Hill helped to finish the church. The ladies and young girls made and embroidered the

kneelers and pew covers, and others gave precious English oak for making new furniture. The vicar engraved Bible pictures on the glass of the windows, using nothing but a dentist's drill! He also made the altar cross, alms-dish and Communion vessels from gifts of old gold, silver and precious stones. These came in the form of rings, trinkets and other pieces of jewellery from many parts of the world. If you turn to page 62 you will see a picture of the inside of St Mark's. It shows the altar or holy table at the east end of the church.

On Saturday, 25th April 1959, the bells rang out for the consecration of the church by the Bishop of Rochester. For many weeks a team of young bellringers had been training to do this. Far more people came than could get into the church. But they were happy that at long last Biggin Hill had a church worthy of God.

We have now had stories of two parish churches, one very old and one very new. You will be able to add yet another story—that of your own parish church (unless *you* happen to live in Biggin Hill or Hartlepool!) Parish churches are there to be used; they are places where God's family meet one another and join in worship and prayer.

> 'In God's quiet house
> We may kneel and pray;
> For we know that he will hear
> Everything we say.'

We can best thank those who built and furnished our lovely churches by using them regularly week by week. Do you use yours?

Things to do

1. Find and mark Biggin Hill on the map.
2. Many new churches have been built in the last few years. Collect any pictures of them you can find to put in your scrapbook.
3. Make up a prayer for St Mark's, Biggin Hill to use; or use this one: 'Heavenly Father, please bless all our churches, both new and old. Bless the clergy and those who lead our worship, and help us all to be quick to learn and keen to do your will, for Jesus' sake. Amen.'

Harder things to do

1. Write a letter to a cousin in New Zealand telling him about 'The Moving Church'.
2. Many people gave precious gifts of gold and silver to the church at Biggin Hill. Look up Acts, chapter 20, verse 35 and write out the words of Jesus. Also read and think about the story in St Luke, chapter 21, verses 1–4.
3. The church was finished because so many people gave their time and their service, as well as their money. Find out if there is any special thing you can do for your own parish church, and then do it.

4 THE BELLS OF THE PARISH CHURCH

We bells have our home in the belfry. Not many people can see us, for we are shielded from wind and storm by the strong walls of our friend, the tower. But if we are rarely seen, our silvery tones are very often heard in the quiet of the countryside or above the noise and din of the busy city.

We call people to worship; in muffled voices we mourn with the sad; sometimes we chime a well-known hymn tune; sometimes we cry out in a merry peal, rejoicing with those who are happy and thankful.

We are made of copper and tin melted together. New members of our family are today made at a bell foundry, but in olden days we were often cast in a temporary furnace built in the churchyard, and people used to throw their silver into the furnace because they thought that would give us a silvery tone! But it is tin we really like, because the tin gives us our musical notes. Before we are hung in the tower we are dedicated at a special service and sometimes given a name. Sometimes we have a verse written upon us. Here are two of them:

> 'I call the living, mourn the dead,
> I tell when days and years are fled,
> For grief and joy, for prayer and praise,
> To heaven my tuneful voice I raise.'

> 'I ring to sermon with a lusty bome
> That all may come, and none may stay at home.'

Perhaps some day the bellringers will bring you up to the belfry to visit us. You may find we are a family of anything up to twelve! Some of our parts have names very like yours. Look now at the picture of the single bell (the great bell of Tong in Shropshire); the part which hangs down inside is the *tongue*, and this hits our thick *lip* when we speak. The narrow part of our body above is called the *waist*; the decorated part above that is called the *shoulder*, and the narrow part at the very top is called the *crown*. You will notice that we are fastened to a wheel with a rope on it; when we are rung the ringers swing us round almost full circle by pulling on the rope. You can see the ringers doing this in the picture of the bells in the tower.

At first we were not very big, as you will see from the other picture in this chapter. It is taken from the Worms Bible of 1148, and shows two men, one blowing a pipe and the other hitting some of us with a hammer to call people to church. On the Continent of Europe we are still chimed by being hit with a hammer.

Here in England you will find us in nearly every parish church. We are not quite sure who is the oldest of our family, but the oldest one with his birthday marked on him lives in the village of Claughton in Cheshire. He was born in the year 1296! The giants of our family mostly live in the Cathedrals. The biggest of us all is Great Paul who lives in the tower of St Paul's in London. He is nearly nine feet high, weighs close on seventeen tons, and has a very loud voice. When he was first taken to London all the other bells rang out to greet him, and he had to travel by night so as not to block the traffic.

Wherever we are, whether we are big or small, many or few, young or old, our job is to call you to worship.

One of us says 'Come! Come! Come! Come!'

Three of us together say '*Come to church! Come to church!*'

Six of us say '*May Jesus Christ be praised!*'

When we are *eight* we say '*Come and worship! Come and worship!*'

We invite all the Lord's people to come to the Lord's house on the Lord's day.

Things to do

1. Draw a picture of bells being rung *or* draw a single bell.
2. Find in your hymnbook the hymn 'When morning gilds the skies' and the verse in it about the church bell. Write out the verse.
3. Here are some Bible words which have been carved on church bells: (1) 'Feed my lambs' (from St John, chapter 21, verse 15); (2) 'Preach the word' (from 2 Timothy, chapter 4, verse 2). Look up the words and find out who first used them and to whom they were addressed.

Harder things to do

1. You will remember what the bells of Bow Church said to Dick Whittington. Try and write a message of the church bells at some of these times: before a service; in the morning; at night; on Christmas Day; on Easter Day; at a wedding; at a funeral.
2. Write out a text or a verse you would like to see inscribed on a new bell.
3. Try to get a group together and learn to ring a set of handbells.

5 *THE FONT*

When we go into a church, the first thing we see is, almost always, the font—the place where people are baptized and so made members of God's family, the Church. A font is really a large basin for holding the water used at baptism. It is put near the church door because it is at the font that we take our first step in the Christian life, being brought there, while still tiny babies, by our parents and godparents.

Fonts are of different shapes and sizes, and usually made of stone, though wood and precious metals are sometimes used too. Many churches have a font shaped rather like that which you can see the children decorating on page 74.

The square-shaped font with a cover on it, which you see on the next page, is world-famous. It is the font of Bridekirk Church in Cumberland and we may imagine its story to be something like this.

One day more than eight hundred years ago the parish priest of Bridekirk was wondering how he could get a new font for his church, when a traveller told him about Richard the Carver. 'He is a famous worker in stone', he said, 'Reginald of Durham told me that he has done some wonderful carvings in the castle at Norham.'

'Then we must have him to make our font', said the priest, and in course of time a font *was* made for Bridekirk by one Richard the Carver, almost certainly the same Richard who worked at Norham.

Let us imagine him happily and cheerfully following his craft in Bridekirk. First, he hewed the great stone into shape. Then he said to himself, 'Now, what shall I carve on the face of the stone? Ah, I know: I will loop a vine all round it. Then when people look at it, perhaps they will remember the words of the Lord Jesus who said "I am the vine and you are the branches", for we are all joined to him at our baptism like the leaves and branches are to the vine.' So Richard carved the vine on the stone. Can you trace its loops on the picture? Then he thought, 'what shall I carve next? . . . Of course, we must have some really ugly faces to frighten the devil away!' So he put them in. You can see them if you look at the top of the picture.

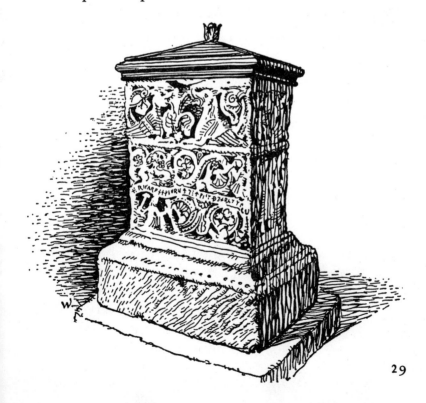

Perhaps next Richard said to himself, 'In days to come
people may wonder what *I* look like! Well then I will
carve myself on the font holding my hammer and chisel.'
So he put himself on the side of the font. You can see
him better in the enlargement on this page. When
Richard had finished his work, he carved across the font
words which when translated mean 'Richard made me,
and with joy he gave me my beauty.'

In the font that Richard made, thousands of babies
have been baptized, and thousands more in the fonts of
other parish churches, including your own. But though so
many of us have been baptized into God's great family,
each one is the child of God, loved by God, and brought
to baptism so that we can learn to love and serve him for
Jesus' sake. Each one is given to the priest, who takes

him (or her) into his arms, and, pouring water over him (or her), says our name and 'I baptize thee in the Name of the Father, and of the Son, and of the Holy Ghost.' That is how God calls each one of us to himself.

In warmer countries baptism often takes place out of doors in a river. You will remember that Jesus himself was baptized in the River Jordan. The picture on this page shows a native African boy being baptized in the river at the Oji River Settlement in Eastern Nigeria. He is one of many who have been cured of leprosy while living at the settlement and has gone back to his home fit and well, and a Christian too.

Wherever we are baptized, whether in a river or at the font in church, what follows after is the same; we are signed with the sign of the Cross in token that 'we shall not be ashamed to confess the faith of Christ crucified, and manfully to fight under his banner against sin, the world and the devil, and to continue Christ's faithful soldiers and servants unto our life's end.'

Things to do

1. Draw the font in your parish church, *or*, if you can't do so, draw one of the fonts in this book.
2. Try to attend a baptism if you have not done so already.
3. Find words like those at the end of the story ('In token that we shall not be ashamed . . .') in the baptism service in your Prayer Book and turn them into a prayer to use yourself.

Harder things to do

1. Find and read these passages in your Bible: St Matthew, chapter 3, verses 13–17; St Matthew, chapter, 28, verses 19 and 20; Acts, chapter 2, verses 37–42; Acts, chapter 8, verses 26–39; Acts, chapter 9, verses 10–18.
   Write down what they tell us about baptism.
2. Read and think about the first four questions and answers in the Church Catechism (the first five in the Revised Catechism).
3. Make a model font from matchboxes *or*
   find a map which marks all the places mentioned in the story of Bridekirk. (You may find one in the A.A. or R.A.C. touring guide.) How many miles would Richard the Carver have to travel to get from Norham to Bridekirk?

6 *THE LECTERN*

If you stand at the back of a church and look towards the chancel, you will see the lectern—a desk or stand with a large Bible on it. The lectern can be on either side of the church, and the reader stands behind it to read the lessons at Morning and Evening Prayer (often called Mattins and Evensong). At each service there are two lessons; one from the first part of the Bible called the Old Testament and one from the New Testament or second part. Can you remember what the lessons were about the last time you went to church?

Some lecterns are very old; and silver, bronze, iron, wood, and stone have all been used in making them. Hardly any two are alike. The picture on this page shows the lectern at Bovey Tracey in Devonshire. You will notice that

the rest or stand for the Bible is made in the shape of an eagle with its wings stretched out for flight. Lecterns made like this remind us of the words of Jesus to his disciples, 'Go ye into all the world and preach the gospel to every creature.' He wanted his gospel to go on wings to every part of the earth. If you look again at the picture you will see that the eagle is standing on a large round ball. I expect you can guess what the ball stands for!

But far more important than the lectern is the book which is upon it—the Holy Bible. We hear it read in church; we can also read it in our own homes. We can go and buy a Bible when we like and where we like, but it was not always so—as you will see from the following story.

Centuries ago—before the days of Guy Fawkes—a great bonfire was lit outside St Paul's Cathedral in London, and on to the bonfire grim-looking bishops and clergy were throwing Bibles! They poked the blaze so that every page should burn, because these Bibles were in English and they didn't believe that ordinary people should have the Bible in their own language, or be able to read it for themselves.

These English Bibles had been translated and printed on the Continent by a young Englishman called William Tyndale. He had fled from England when the Church leaders tried to stop him doing this work. But the more Bibles they burnt, the more he printed. They were smuggled into England, hidden in bales of cloth and sacks of flour! Soon hundreds of people in England were secretly reading their Bibles in a language they could understand. William Tyndale went on with his work

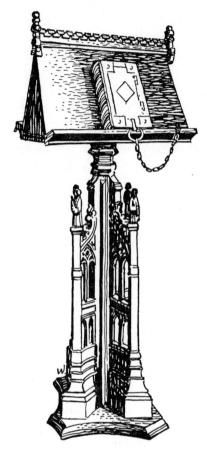

until at last he was betrayed by a trick and burnt at the stake. His last prayer was 'Lord, open the King of England's eyes.' Two years later his prayer was wonderfully answered when King Henry the Eighth ordered a large Bible in English to be placed in every parish church. As these Bibles were still very precious, they were chained to the lectern so that they couldn't be carried away. Our picture on the page shows a chained Bible on the lectern at Ramsey, Huntingdonshire.

All this happened long ago. Today, although we can each have our own Bible and read it for ourselves, we still listen to it being read to us in church—to *the lessons*, God's lessons for us. Here is a prayer which some people repeat to themselves at the time the lessons are read:

'Holy Spirit, help me to listen;
Holy Spirit, help me to understand;
Holy Spirit, help me to remember.'

Things to do

1. Draw the lectern in your own church *or* one of those in this book.
2. Act or mime scenes in the life of William Tyndale.
3. Learn the prayer at the end of the story ('Holy Spirit, help me . . .)
4. Copy and colour the words about the Bible in Psalm 119, verse 105. (Use your Prayer Book to find this.)

Harder things to do

1. Find in your Prayer Book the places in Morning and Evening Prayer where the lessons are mentioned, and see what is said about them.
2. Find in your Bible and read St Luke, chapter 4, verses 16–20. Who read the lesson? Where did he read it? From what book? Who heard the lesson? (If you look up Isaiah, chapter 61, verses 1 and 2 you will find there the lesson that was read.)
3. Read the Bible regularly with the help of daily notes. You can get these through your parish church. The Collect for the Second Sunday in Advent is about the Bible. Read the Collect, talk about it, try to understand it and then use it yourself in your own prayers.

7   *THE PULPIT*

Every parish church has its pulpit—the place from which sermons are preached. You can see from the picture on

this page that the preacher, when he is in the pulpit, is higher up than the congregation. That is so that he can be seen and heard more easily.

Many pulpits are made of stone, but there are some fine wooden ones too. You may like to know the story of the pulpit in the church of Marr, near Doncaster. The picture of it is on page 39.

The letters CB, which you can see, stand for Christopher Barker, who was born nearly four hundred and fifty years ago in the vicarage at Marr. As a boy he went to church Sunday by Sunday with his family. When he grew up he went to London, like Dick Whittington, to seek his fortune, and no doubt he often thought about his home and church in Marr and what he had learned there.

'If ever I become a rich man', he said, 'I will make a handsome gift to the church I love. That will be the best way of saying "thank you" to God for all his goodness.'

Christopher's ambition had always been to print Bibles, and to print them better than they had ever been printed before. Like William Tyndale, about whom we read in chapter 6, he lived in times when Bibles were scarce and precious, and when English people wanted them and couldn't get them. But when he got to London, he found it wasn't at all easy to become a Bible-printer, so he started to sell them instead, in the meantime keeping a sharp look-out for a printing business he could buy.

At last his chance came; he bought some printing works and 'in Paul's Churchyard at the sign of the Tiger's Head' he printed his first Bibles. Soon afterwards he became official printer to Queen Elizabeth the First and then all the Bibles printed in English were printed by him.

Christopher Barker was now rich and famous, with a large house in London and another near Windsor, but he did not forget Marr or the thankoffering he had promised to the church; and so one day he made up his mind to return to the village of his childhood and there offer his gift. We can imagine Christopher, his wife, and his sons Christopher and Robert, setting off on the long slow journey to Yorkshire. They most likely travelled in a handsome coach pulled by a team of horses and with pages and servants in attendance. Each night they would stay at one of the many wayside inns on the Great North Road.

When they reached Marr, Christopher Barker told the

vicar who he was and why he had come. 'I should like to make a gift', he said, 'to the church in which I worshipped as a boy and where I first learned to know and love God. Of course you shall have one of my best Bibles, but I would like to give something else too.'

'It is indeed kind of you', said the vicar, 'I greatly need a pulpit from which to speak to the people about the Lord Jesus.'

'That you shall certainly have', said Christopher, and so he hunted out a woodworker who lived near to make and carve a pulpit for Marr church. In the picture you can see Christopher Barker showing his wife the finished pulpit. He is pointing to his initials and his coat of arms. I expect young Christopher and Robert liked the pulpit too!

The Bible which Christopher Barker gave to the church of Marr was large and beautifully bound. The front of it was covered by a plate of fine brass on which the name of the man who gave it was written, and also the year— 1579. The Bible has long since disappeared but you can still see the pulpit in the church today—just as it was when first put there nearly four hundred years ago.

Christopher Barker came to know and love God through going to church from the time he was quite a small boy. It is that way still for boys and girls and everyone today; God makes himself known to us through the services of the Church—through the *lessons*, when the Word of God is read from the Old Testament and the New Testament, and through the *sermon*, when the Word of God is preached from the pulpit. So we *must listen*!

40

Things to do

1. Draw, describe or make a model of the pulpit in your parish church.
2. Make up a strip cartoon of scenes from the life of Christopher Barker.
3. Copy out and learn St Mark, chapter 16, verse 15.

Harder things to do

1. Write out the words your rector or vicar uses before he begins his sermon.
2. Look up and read these three passages in your Bible: St Matthew, chapter 5, verses 1–12; St Mark, chapter 4, verses 1–9; St Matthew, chapter 24, verses 3–14. Find from each of them where our Lord preached; what he preached about; and who listened to what he said. After next Sunday add to your notes where your rector or vicar preached; what he preached about; and who listened to what he said.
3. A sermon generally has a text—that is, a verse from the Bible. Choose a suitable text for a sermon for (1) Easter Day, (2) Christmas Day, (3) Ash Wednesday, (4) Ascension Day, (5) Whitsunday.

8 *THE LITANY DESK*

When you stand at the back of a church and look up the aisle—that is the name given to the passageway between the pews—you will sometimes see in the middle of it a prayer desk. It is called the Litany desk, and the book upon it is called *The Litany*, as you will see from the picture on this page.

Litanies are 'asking prayers', said partly by the priest and partly by the people. We know prayers like these from our day school assembly and Sunday school worship; as when someone says 'Let us pray for all those that are sick, especially those known to us', and we answer all together, 'Lord, hear our prayer.' The Litany in our Prayer Book is all made up in this way, as you can see for yourself if you look it up.

To know how church litanies started we have to go back many centuries to a town called Vienne in the South of France, where there was once a terrible earthquake. It killed many people, houses and buildings came crashing down and the crops were ruined in the fields. The people were very frightened; they thought that still more earthquakes would follow and then there would be famine too; so their bishop, Mamertus, said to them, 'We will have three special days of prayer, and we will walk in procession through our towns, asking God to spare them from further destruction.'

So the people got ready. Boys and girls put on their strongest shoes; the clergy polished their crosses of silver and brass which they were to carry in the procession, and they saw that their robes were clean. Bishop Mamertus and the people carried out their plan on the three days before Ascension Day, and these days came to be known as 'Rogation' or asking days.

Many years afterwards, when all fear of earthquakes had been forgotten, the people of Vienne still had their processions and sang their prayers out of doors as their fathers had done before them. Among the prayers they sang were these:

> 'O God the Father, have mercy upon us,
> O God the Son, have mercy upon us,
> O God the Holy Ghost, have mercy upon us.'

These special prayers they called *The Litany*.

The custom of singing *the Litany* out of doors spread from France to England. Our picture shows the clergy leaving the cathedral church of Ely on one of these processions. Everyone used to join in—bishop, priests, monks and nuns, grown-ups and children. English boys and girls loved this kind of service, and though it was sung in Latin they were able to join in at the 'Have mercy upon us' part.

In the reign of Henry the Eighth *the Litany* was put into English; everyone then could understand and join in better. After a time the people ceased to sing *the Litany* in procession so much, and got into the habit of kneeling for it in church, as we generally do now; but on the three Rogation Days they still kept up the custom of a procession round the parish. It was called 'beating the bounds'. We can see why they did so. They wanted to call down God's blessing on all the homes, farms, fields, shops and industries of their parish.

The Litany desk is placed in the nave of the church where the people sit, to remind them that the Litany prayers are specially the people's prayers: for themselves, their Church, their country, their homes and their friends. *The Litany* helps us to remember to pray for others; it also shows us one good way of doing this together.

Things to do

1. Draw the litany desk in your own church *or* the one in this book.
2. Act the story of Mamertus and the people of Vienne.
3. Write out and learn by heart the two chief responses in the Litany.

Harder things to do

1. Find out from your Prayer Book when the Litany is to be used, and also another name for it. ('The Ordinary' means the bishop.)
2. Can you find the words from the Litany of Vienne in our Prayer Book Litany? (Formerly 'miserable' meant not 'sad' but 'to be pitied'. 'Miserable sinners' means 'sinners who need pity'.)
3. Find in the Litany the places where we pray for: (1) the Queen; (2) the clergy; (3) the sick; (4) refugees; (5) our enemies.
4. In the story we read about an earthquake at Vienne many hundreds of years ago. There have been earthquakes in our own life-time also. See if you can find out where they took place and what happened to the people and their homes. Write about them in your notebook and get pictures, or draw some, if you can. What can we do for people who suffer through earthquakes?
5. Find and read I Timothy, chapter 2, verse 1. What do you think St Paul would have said if Timothy had gone to him with a Litany?

9 *THE PRAYER DESK*

In our tour of the church we have now visited the font, the lectern, the litany desk and the pulpit. Somewhere near the lectern or the pulpit we shall find the priest's stall or prayer desk. It is generally inside the chancel as it is in the picture on page 48, but in some churches it is found in the nave nearer the people. The priest goes to this stall for the services of Morning and Evening Prayer, or, as they are often called, Mattins and Evensong.

You may like to know the story of a certain Sunday morning not long ago when a most unusual visitor attended Mattins in a country church. The visitor was a sparrow! He flew in through the open door and round and round the church and then perched on the highest rafters. There he found a bat just wakening up from his long winter's sleep.

'What are you doing here?' said the bat.

'The door was open', said the sparrow, 'and I thought I would just come in and explore. I've often wondered what this place was like inside.'

'Hush', said the bat, 'they're coming in for the service. I've seen them often. You see I have lived here a long time.'

From his perch the sparrow watched the service below. When the people knelt down and said, 'We have erred and strayed from thy ways like lost sheep', the sparrow whispered, 'What are they doing now?'

'They are talking to the Heavenly Father who made us all, telling him they are sorry for all the wrong things they have done.'

'There is a man standing up', said the sparrow.

'Yes', replied his friend, 'that is the parish priest; he leads the worship of the people. He is standing in his stall, telling the people that God forgives all who are truly sorry for their wrongdoing.'

Then the sparrow saw everyone stand up, and soon the organ played and the people praised God. The music made the little fellow very happy and he joined in with his best bird songs, chirruping away for all he was worth. Then the music stopped. The sparrow watched, then whispered to the bat, 'That man—parish priest you called him—has walked from his place and is reading from a big book.'

The bat answered, 'That book is the Bible, and the stand it is on is the lectern.'

So the sparrow watched and listened: there was more singing, then more reading and more singing again. Then the people knelt down and the sparrow whispered to his friend, 'What are they doing now? Are they saying they are sorry again?'

'No', he replied, 'they are praying to God, who loves all men, for the Queen, for their friends, for those in need and for themselves.'

Then, a little later, the sparrow said, 'Look, the parish priest is going to another place.'

'Yes', said the bat, 'that is the pulpit. You watch; the people will sit down and he will talk to them.'

The sparrow listened and heard the parish priest say 'God has made everything; he knows everything; not even a sparrow can fall to the ground without his leave.' When the little sparrow heard himself mentioned he said, 'Now I will let them see me!' and he flew round and round the church. The choir boys grinned and nudged each other as they watched, and then back went the little visitor to his perch beside the bat. Later on he saw the parish priest go to another place—the holy table or altar—and there put up his hand in blessing. Then everyone went out.

As the church was emptying the bat said, 'If I were you I should fly out before they close the doors.'

'What about you?' said the sparrow.

'I shall have a fly round myself after everyone has gone, to stretch my wings a bit.'

So the sparrow flew out into the sunshine. He never

forgot the morning when he joined in the service called Mattins. Nor did he forget the parish priest who had done so much in the service to lead the praises, prayers and worship of God's people.

Things to do

1. Make a drawing or a model of a priest's stall; if you can, of that in your own church.
2. The priest in the picture is wearing cassock, surplice, hood and scarf. If you do not know already, get a friend to show you which is which.
3. Draw the priest and choir going into church for Mattins as the sparrow saw them when he looked down from the rafters.

Harder things to do

1. Find St Matthew, chapter 10, verses 29–31 in your Bible. What do we learn from these verses about sparrows; about ourselves?
2. In the picture the priest is reading the Absolution. Can you find this in the Prayer Book and say what 'absolution' means. (Use your dictionary if necessary.) Then write out how the bat described it.
3. Make a list of those parts of Morning Prayer which can be said or sung, *and* learn 'The Grace' with which Morning Prayer and Evening Prayer end.

IO THE ORGAN

In most parish churches the organ is the largest piece of furniture; you will know it by the rows of pipes in front, like those you see in the picture on page 53. Let us first answer the question that boys and girls often ask about the organ: 'What is it like inside, and how does it work?'

If we could climb inside we should find there a whole forest of pipes of all shapes and sizes. Some are as large as pillars and some no bigger than a recorder. Some are straight and some are crooked. There are fat pipes, slender pipes, open pipes and stopped pipes. Some— the big ones—can growl like thunder and seem to make the whole building shake. Others—the little ones— make sounds that remind us of birds singing on a spring morning. Some of the pipes make sounds like your voices when you sing; some are like the deep voices of grown-up men. Some whisper like flutes, some wail like violins and some give a great roar like a trumpet.

Behind the pipes are bellows which are filled with wind by an electric motor. When the organist plays a note he lets wind into the pipe belonging to that note and it 'speaks'—just as your recorder or tin whistle 'speaks' when you blow through it.

Each single note has many pipes linked to it and the organist can play one, two, three, or all of them at once by simply pulling out or pushing in the 'stops' at each side of or in front of him. You will see that these have the names of the pipes written on them.

An organ has one, two, three or more keyboards according to its size, with black and white keys like a

piano, and further, if you look below the organ stool you will see that the organist has a keyboard for his feet too!

In earlier times organs were much simpler, as we can see from the picture on this page. It is drawn from a

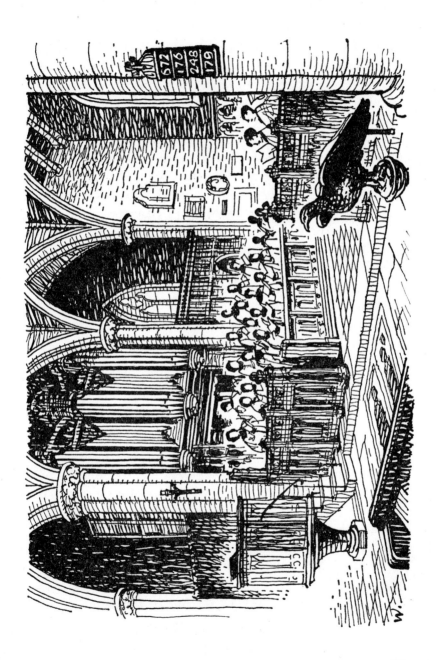

stained-glass window in the church of Merevale in Worcestershire. Here the organ is so small that it can be carried. The man is walking along playing with his left hand and blowing the wind in with his right!

The organ is sometimes called the 'King of Instruments' because it can make so many different sounds, separately or together. But it cannot make these sounds by itself; it needs an organist to play it. There are more organs than organists in our parish churches today; if boys and girls who are learning to play the piano would learn to play an organ too they would be able to serve God in a special way by helping God's people to praise him.

Even if you are not learning an instrument you can still help by becoming a chorister in the church choir, and so helping to lead the praises of God's people. There is plenty of room for those who want to use their voices to sing praise to God, and plenty of music to sing. Some of the lovelist music in the world was written to be played and sung in English churches.

Sometimes in church, people grow lazy and let the organ do all the work. But wonderful as it is, the organ is only a machine, and if we are silent when we ought to be singing, if we think the organ is making enough noise and we need not bother, we are doing wrong. God wants *our* praise; he misses it when it is not given and the organ does not make up for it. When we do join in the praises of God, we are giving something that is our very own, and that is what God likes best of all. Perhaps you would like to learn these words from Psalm 103:

Praise the Lord, O my soul: and all that
is within me praise his holy Name.

Things to do

1. Make a drawing of the organ in your parish church.
2. Copy in colour and learn by heart the last verse of Psalm 150.
3. Unjumble the letters to find the question; then answer it: Sing, or play and sing the SRVEE you EIKL best in your EIAVUORFT NYMH.

Harder things to do

1. Make a list of all the places where the organ plays at *one* of the services you attend.
2. Find the 'music' verse in each of these hymns and copy out the one you like best: 'O praise ye the Lord'; 'Angels voices ever singing'; 'O come all ye faithful'; 'God of mercy, God of grace'. Sing it as a solo if you can.
3. Listen to a record of an organist playing Bach's Toccata and Fugue in D Minor.
4. Find in your Bible and read Ephesians, chapter 5, verses 19 and 20. You will then know what St Paul says about music in our worship. Can you think of three places in the Holy Communion service *or* in Morning and Evening Prayer where we follow St Paul's advice? (In your answer leave out anything from the hymnbook.)
5. Learn to play an organ.

II THE BISHOP'S CHAIR

Two boys, called Robert and John, were walking by a church in a town where they lived when they saw a large notice outside the church door. It said 'Confirmation tonight at 7 p.m.' It was a bright, cheerful-looking poster. They stopped to see how it had been done. While they stood there, along came the vicar just in time to hear Robert say to John, 'I wonder what that's all about'.

'Would you like to know?' said the vicar.

'Yes', they both replied.

'Very well. Come into church with me and I will tell you.'

They all sat down in one of the pews and the vicar said, 'It really all started in the first days of the Church. Has anyone ever told you how the Church started?'

John said, 'We had a lesson at school before the holidays about the Holy Spirit coming to the apostles. Is that what you mean?'

'Yes', said the vicar, 'that was the birthday of the Church—which we remember every year on Whitsunday. Those followers of Jesus didn't keep the Holy Spirit to themselves; they went out to tell the glad news to anyone who would listen, and soon lots of people joined the Church. Then the apostles chose some keen young men to help them in their work. One of them was called Philip. He said, "I would like to go to Samaria and preach about Jesus there. It isn't very far—only thirty-five miles." So Philip went and very soon many

56

people in Samaria became followers of Jesus and were baptized.'

'When this news reached the apostles in Jerusalem, they were very glad. They said, "Some of us ought to go to Samaria and lay our hands on the people Philip has baptized; then they will receive the Holy Spirit." Peter and John were chosen to go. When they reached Samaria, they prayed for the new Christians and laid their hands on them and they received the Holy Spirit.'

'That is what is happening in our church tonight', the vicar explained. 'The bishop is coming to do just what the apostles did; he will lay his hands on all those who are to be confirmed, so that they may receive the gift of the Holy Spirit.'

'Can anybody come to the service?'asked Robert.

'Yes', said the vicar, 'I hope you will both come and see for yourselves.' The two boys thanked the vicar and promised to come to the service.

There were already people in church when Robert and John got there. They were just in time to see two choirmen carry the bishop's chair from its place by the side of the altar to the chancel entrance. You can see this in the picture on page 58. Then those who were to be confirmed came and sat in the front seats. The men and boys were on one side, and the women and girls were on the other. The women and girls all wore white veils.

The service began, and the bishop asked those who had come to be confirmed if they would try to keep the promises made in their name at their baptism by their godfathers and godmothers. They said they would. Then the two boys saw the bishop do just what Peter and John did when they went to Samaria. First he prayed for the candidates, then he confirmed them by laying his hands on each of them in turn. (You can see a bishop doing this in the picture on page 59.) As he confirmed each one the bishop said, 'Defend, O Lord, this thy Child with thy heavenly grace, that he may continue thine for ever; and daily increase in thy Holy Spirit, more and more, until he come to thy everlasting kingdom. Amen.'

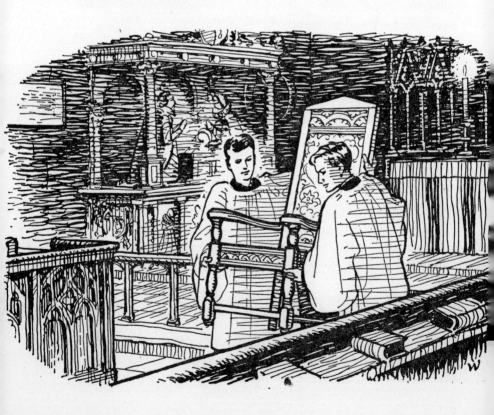

As they went home Robert and John talked about the service. They decided that when they were older, they too would ask to be confirmed.

Things to do

1. Draw the chair which Robert and John saw, *or* the chair the bishop is sitting on, *or* best of all, the bishop's chair in your own church.
2. If you haven't yet done so, attend a Confirmation.
3. Collect any pictures you can find of your own bishop and paste them into your scrapbook.

Harder things to do

1. Find in your Bible and read Acts, chapter 8, verses 4–17. Read it from the *New English Bible* if you can. Write down what you think Philip would tell the people of Samaria about Jesus.
2. Turn to the Confirmation service in the Prayer Book.
    (a) Find in it the words 'come to years of discretion' and write down what they mean.
    (b) Find the place in the service where the bishop speaks about the first Confirmation in Samaria.
    (c) Find what it says about the Holy Communion.
3. Find in your hymnbook the hymns for use at a Confirmation, and write out a verse from the hymn you like best.

12 THE LORD'S TABLE OR ALTAR

The most important piece of furniture in our church is called the Lord's table, or altar. It is generally to be found at the east end of the church, and is in the middle where everyone can see it. The railed-off part in which the altar stands is called the *Sanctuary*. Behind the altar there is often a picture or piece of carved work on the wall. This is called the *Reredos*. You can see a picture of the reredos of St Mark's, Biggin Hill, on the next page. Many parish churches have more than one holy table or altar, especially those which have side chapels.

The priest goes to the altar for the service of Holy Communion. It is the chief of all our services and the one which Jesus himself gave to his Church. This is the story of how it happened.

On the morning before he was crucified, Jesus was going towards Jerusalem with his disciples, when one of them said, 'It will soon be time for the Passover Feast. Where are we going to have *our* Passover meal?'

Jesus then sent two disciples on in front. 'Go straight into the city', he said, 'and you will see a man carrying a jar of water on his head. Follow him and he will take you to an upstairs room. Get everything ready for us there.'

The two disciples went on ahead, and did as they were asked, and in the evening Jesus came to this upstairs room along with the rest of his twelve companions.

It had been a tiring day and the disciples were quarrel-some. They kept on arguing about which of them should be first. Jesus very quietly took off his coat, put water in a dish and fastened a towel round his waist. Then he washed his disciples' feet and dried them on the towel. He did this for each of them in turn; then he put his coat on again and came and sat down. He said, 'Do you know what I have just done to you? You call me "Master" and "Lord", and you are quite right, for that is what I am. Yet, you see, I have been doing the work of a servant for you, and have given you an example so that you may do as I have done.'

Then they had their meal together. After it was over Jesus took some of the bread that was left, into his hands. He gave thanks to God the Father and then broke the bread into pieces. He gave some of it to each of his disciples, saying as he did so, 'Take, eat, this is my Body which is given for you.' Then he took into his hands a cup with wine in it and once again he gave thanks to God the Father. He gave the cup to his disciples and said, 'Drink of this; for this is my Blood which is shed for you. Go on doing this in remembrance of me.' You can see Jesus holding the cup in his hands in the picture on the next page.

At the time the disciples did not understand what this meant. But on the next day, which was Good Friday, Jesus gave his life on the cross. His precious Body was broken and his precious Blood was shed for all men, and I expect then the disciples began to understand a little bit better about the Last Supper and what Jesus meant when he said 'This is my Body'; 'This is my Blood.'

After Jesus rose from the dead, the disciples went on

doing what their Master had told them to do in remembrance of him. They felt then that he was very near them, even though they could no longer see him with their naked eyes.

All through the ages whenever Christians have gathered together, they have broken the bread and shared the cup in the Holy Communion, which is often called the Lord's own service. You can see this happening in the picture on this page.

Things to do

1. Draw the holy table or altar as it is in your parish church, and make a list of everything else you can see in the sanctuary.
2. Find the service, known as 'The Lord's Own Service', in your Prayer Book and write down its two titles. This will help you

   T _ _   L _ _ _ _   S _ _ _ _ _

   H _ _ _   C _ _ _ _ _ _ _ _

3. Write down what Jesus said about the bread he broke, and what he said about the wine he blessed.

Harder things to do

1. Look up, read and compare these places in the New Testament. They all tell the story of the upper room and the Last Supper: St Matthew, chapter 26, verses 17–30; St Mark, chapter 14, verses 12–26; St Luke, chapter 22, verses 1–30; St John, chapter 13, verses 1–15; 1 Corinthians, chapter 11, verses 23–26.
2. Find and read Acts, chapter 20, verses 6–8. Which was 'the first day of the week'? Why did they 'break bread'—that is have their Holy Communion—on that day?
3. Look carefully at the picture of the reredos at St Mark's, Biggin Hill. Can you say what it means? If you find this hard, get a grown-up to help you.

13 *THE HOLY COMMUNION*

Do you remember the story of the sparrow who attended Mattins one Sunday in a country church? (It was told in chapter 9.) Some months later, he had another adventure. He flew off into the town one day and found himself near a church. It was Sunday; the bells were ringing, the church door was open and so he went in. He flew round and round among the rafters looking for a friendly bat, but none could he find. So he settled down to watch. 'I shall not have anybody to tell me about the service this time', he said to himself.

He soon knew that he had come to a different sort of service. When the choir came in the priest did not go to his prayer desk but to the holy table or altar, and with him went two servers. You can see the procession as the sparrow saw it in the picture on the next page.

There was some singing and there were prayers, and then more singing, but the little sparrow did not understand it much. Then everyone stood up, and the sparrow got very excited because he heard the priest say, 'Behold the fowls of the air; for they sow not, neither do they reap, nor gather into barns; yet your heavenly Father feedeth them.' But he didn't fly round and show himself as he had done before. He kept very quiet and went on watching.

Then he saw the priest go to the pulpit. 'That is what he did in the other service', the sparrow said to himself, 'I wonder if he is going to talk about me now?' And he

got ready to fly round. The sparrow listened very hard, but the priest didn't talk about him. He talked about the service in which they were all taking part.

'In this service', he said, 'we do again what the Lord did at the Last Supper. We break the bread and bless the cup as he said we should, so that those who eat of the bread and drink of the cup may be strengthened by the Body and Blood of Christ. That is what we share when we kneel at the altar.'

After the sermon there was a hymn and the little sparrow saw offerings being taken to the priest—of money, bread and wine. Then, as he watched, the people knelt down. Then followed more prayers and more singing which he didn't understand, but he liked one piece of music very much. It was the music to the words 'Holy, holy, holy, Lord God of hosts, heaven and earth are full of the glory. Glory be to thee, O Lord most High.' During this music he chirped away to his heart's content.

Next he saw the priest take the bread and wine into his hands and consecrate them. Soon the people were coming up to the communion rail to share in the Body and Blood of Christ. The sparrow thought the service was nearly over when he saw people moving about, and he was so frightened of being shut in the church, that he left his safe seat up in the rafters and flew out into the summer sunshine! He missed the end of the service when priest and people thanked God for the wonderful gift of the Body and Blood of Christ. He also missed the chance of joining in the great hymn of thanksgiving 'Glory be to God on high.'

Our parish churches follow different customs and traditions in the Holy Communion service. It is called by different titles. One is the 'Eucharist'. which means 'thanksgiving'. Another is the 'Lord's Supper', as in the Prayer Book. Another very old name for the service is

the 'Mass'. Sometimes the priest is dressed as you see him on page 70; sometimes as he is in the picture on page 65. But these are only outward differeneces. It is still the same service, in which the Lord Jesus comes in his love and power to share his life with all who seek to serve and follow him.

Things to do

1. Write out and learn the words 'Holy, holy, holy' down to 'O Lord most High.' Learn them to use in your prayers. Learn the music too if you can.
2. The dish used for the bread in Holy Communion is called a *paten*. The cup is challed a *chalice*. Draw each of these and write the special name beside each one.
3. Draw your own church ready for Holy Communion as the sparrow might see it if he were to fly in next Sunday.

Harder things to do

1. Write down in order what happens at the Holy Communion service you attend.
2. The sparrow visited the town church on one of the Sundays after Trinity. Find out which Sunday it was.
3. Learn the hymn 'Glory be to God on high', and use it in your prayers.
4. Why is the Holy Communion service often called the chief service in our Church?

14 *HELPERS IN THE PARISH CHURCH*

Many people help in the parish church. We have already mentioned bellringers, organists, choristers and servers. But there are others too whom we must not forget. They all do special work.

The *churchwardens* help and advise the parish priest, show people to their seats and look after the church. There are generally two churchwardens; they have a staff or wand of office which they sometimes carry in processions. Then there are the *sidesmen*. They help the churchwardens in seating the people, give out the books and sometimes take the collection. The *sexton* or *verger* does all kinds of odd jobs round the church and church-yard; sometimes, though not always, he (or she) is cleaner and caretaker as well.

In every parish there is a *Parochial Church Council*. Its members are elected every year at a special meeting. The parish priest is the chairman of the council. Its main task is to help the parish priest in his work in the church and in the parish. Members of the church council give of their time, their talents and their money to God's work, and try to show an example to other people in the parish by their Christian witness and Christian service.

These are some of the ways in which grown-up people help their parish church. But boys and girls can help too. We will put first being in your places in church on Sunday—in the Lord's house on the Lord's day—and giving something from your own pocket-money for God's work. All who go to church regularly show other people that they belong to Jesus and want to love and follow him. In our services the Lord Jesus comes to us with his help and love. He once said 'Where two or three are gathered in my name, there am I in the midst of them.'

The pictures in this chapter show other ways of helping. The first picture shows two boys and a girl getting things ready for Evensong. One boy is lighting the candles, one is bringing in the books and the girl is busy opening the books at their right places.

At special times in the year the church is decorated

with flowers and greenery, and here, too, boys and girls can give welcome help. You will see in the picture on this page some children helping a grown-up to decorate the font. Sometimes, after the Harvest Festival for instance, gifts are sent from the church to the old and infirm, and boys and girls take the parcels round as you see them doing in the picture on the page opposite.

A boy called John Brown once went from his parish church with a basket of groceries for an old lady called Mrs Simpson. 'These are from St Peter's', he said.

'Thank you very much', was the reply, 'do come in.'

John and Mrs Simpson soon became fast friends, and he often went to help her; going messages, getting in the coal and doing all sorts of odd jobs, and Mrs Simpson generally had some little thing for John too. One day as they were talking, Mrs Simpson said 'It is good of you to come and help me; perhaps you come sometimes when you would rather go out and play.'

'I would rather go and play sometimes', said John, 'but all of us at St Peter's try to follow Jesus by helping others, especially those who want it most.'

'I am sure that the Lord Jesus has a smile and a welcome for all who follow him like that', said Mrs Simpson, 'I will tell you how I know. . . .'

Things to do

1. Write down the names of the churchwardens of your parish church, and draw a picture of their wands of office.
2. Make a list of the ways you have helped or are helping your church.
3. Draw a picture of boys and girls giving some kind of help to their parish church: *or* make a strip cartoon of pictures telling the story of John Brown and Mrs Simpson.

Harder things to do

1. Mrs Simpson said, 'I will tell you how I know'. What she did then was to take down her Bible and find St Matthew, chapter 25, verses 31–40. Find and read these words for yourself and try to imagine what Mrs Simpson and John might say to each other. Then write it down.
2. Read 1 Corinthians, chapter 16, verses 1 and 2. Would St Paul agree with us putting something by each week for God's work?
3. Find out how much money is given to your church each year and what it is spent on. You will need grown-ups to help you to do this.

15 *THE CATHEDRAL*

Your parish and parish church is part of a *diocese*, which may include as many as four or five hundred parishes. Every diocese has a mother church or cathedral, and there the bishop has his seat. Many of our cathedrals are famous churches with an exciting story of their own. Here is the story of one of them—the mother church or cathedral of the Diocese of Ely.

'Look', said Queen Etheldreda to Se-wenna her serving-maid, 'yonder is Ely, my own country. We have reached our journey's end; our weeks of travelling are over.'

Etheldreda had returned from far Northumbria to Ely to build a church and found a monastery. She and her friends wanted to live the life of monks and nuns, serving God in study, prayer and worship. The queen had chosen Ely because in those far-off days it was almost an island. All round it were rivers, swamps and trackless bogs. She felt she would be safe in Ely from any sudden attack by an enemy.

Soon the building of the monastery church was finished. You can see Etheldreda with her work-people in the picture on the next page. She became the first abbess. Every day, week in and week out, worship was offered to God in the great church, and it went on long after Etheldreda died. Then, a hundred years later, a great disaster overtook Ely. Over the fens came 'a mighty heathen host' of Danes and Norsemen. They plundered

and burned down the monastery and put most of the monks to death.

The fire-swept ruins of the great church were silent; no daily worship was now offered. But it was not to be like this for long. Eight priests had escaped from the cruel Norsemen. They met together secretly.

'Let us wait till our enemies have gone', said one, 'they will soon grow tired of living in Ely, and then we can go back.'

'Yes', said another, 'and perhaps we can rebuild one bit of our church and worship God there like we used to.'

And that was what happened; the little band of faithful priests began again to worship God in the ruined church. A hundred years later their faithfulness was rewarded. The monastery was restored and new life came to the church in Ely.

There is a story that one Candlemas Day the great King Canute was approaching the city in his barge, when he heard the sounds of lovely music floating across the air. 'What is that?' he asked. 'It is the monks singing the evening service', was the reply.

Then Canute himself made up a song with these words:

Sweetly sang the monks of Ely
As Canute the king sailed by:
Soldiers, row me near the spire
That we may hear the angelic choir.

After that the king often came to Ely and gave many rich gifts to the church.

After another hundred years Abbot Simeon began the present cathedral. You can see it on the next page as it looks today from the air. It was not all built at once. Three hundred years were to pass before it was finished. Try to imagine what a task it was! All the wood and stone had to come many miles along the twisting waterways in boats and barges. There were no hard roads in those days. Some workmen went to Barnack, thirty miles away, to cut out great blocks of stone in the quarries; others felled giant oaks in the forest. Roads and bridges and the river banks had all to be made stronger so as to bear the extra weight of great cartloads of stone.

The story of our cathedrals, like the story of our parish churches, is a story of many faithful people. They all played their part. We too play our part today as members of God's family. Our church looks to us to help in every way we can.

Things to do

1. Write down the name of your diocese and try to get pictures of your cathedral for your scrapbook. If you have not been to see your cathedral, try and arrange to visit it.
2. There are several scenes in this story for you to draw. You may like to do a 'strip cartoon' of pictures showing the life of Etheldreda.
3. Write out and learn the first two verses of the hymn 'We love the place, O God'.

Harder things to do

1. Ask a grown-up to help you to find a book included in some Bibles called Ecclesiasticus. In chapter 38, verses 24–34 there is a good description of different kinds of craftsmen who serve God in their daily work. Read this passage and, if you have time, make drawings of the workmen described.
2. See if you can find out how cathedrals came to be called by the name 'cathedral'.
3. Here is an old monastery prayer to learn and use: 'Preserve us, O Lord, while waking, and guard us

while sleeping, that awake we may watch with Christ, and asleep we may rest in peace.' Also look up and think about the hymn 'Before the ending of the day', which was probably sung in the monastery church of Ely in Etheldreda's day.

THE SEASONS IN
OUR CHURCH

*Read these chapters at the time
when the seasons they are about
come round*

16   *ADVENT*

In this part of our book we are to think about the seasons of the Christian year as they are observed in our parish church. A year can start at any time. Your birthday starts a new year in your life. At school the new year begins after the summer holidays. Our diaries start a new year on 1st January. The Church's year starts about a month before that, *on the First Sunday in Advent.*

'Advent' means coming, and in Advent we think about the coming of Jesus and how God got ready for it; preparing the way through the prophets, through John the Baptist and through the message of the Angel Gabriel to the Blessed Virgin Mary. So, among other things, Advent is our 'getting ready' season, when we get ready for Christmas and for all the other fasts and festivals which follow in the course of the year.

Sometimes boys and girls find it hard to remember the order in which the fasts and festivals come. They are like Anne, who cried out one night, 'Oh, I shall never remember these Church names!' She was trying to find a Sunday collect in her Prayer Book. Just then her brother John, who was seventeen, looked up from his homework. 'If you wait till I'm finished', he said, 'I will show you something to help you to find your places quickly.'

When John had finished his homework he went to get the chart which you can see on the opposite page.

THE CHRISTIAN YEAR

'There you are', he said, 'I have just finished that for my Sunday school class.'

'Tell us about it', said young William, who went with his sister Anne to look at John's picture.

'Well', said John, 'it is meant to show all the chief Christian seasons in their right order. What is between one little doorway and the next is a whole year.'

'I can't read all those long words', said young William. So John read them over to him.

'Why have you made all those ups and downs?' asked Anne.

'I had to do that', said John, 'because I wanted to get the great days of the Christian year on to high places and that meant I had to have hollows as well. You can't have hills without hollows.'

After looking at the picture for a while Anne said, 'I suppose that the great days are Christmas, Easter, Ascension, Whitsun and Trinity—that is five.'

'That's right', said John.

Then Anne asked, 'Why have you written three names underneath?'

'Because', said John, 'they are all "getting ready" times as well as being useful in themselves. Just as Advent is a "get ready" time for Christmas, so Lent is a "get ready" time for Easter; and many people think that the three Rogation days prepare us for Ascensiontide and Whitsunday.'

' Can I copy that on to a little piece of paper and put it in my Prayer Book?' asked Anne, 'then I can learn the seasons in the right order.'

'Yes', said John, 'and while you are busy, you can put in the missing figures at each end of the chart.'

Things to do

1. Make your own copy of John's chart.
2. Write these two lines in your note book.

> 'With ADVENT starts the Church's year
> Proclaiming that our Lord is near.'

(Start at the top of the page and leave the whole page below and the next one blank. There will be other lines to add underneath later on.)

3. What special colour is used in your church during Advent? Copy and colour

ADVENT

in the right Advent colour.

Harder things to do

1. These lessons from the Old Testament are read during Advent—Isaiah, chapter 9, verses 2, 6 and 7; Isaiah, chapter 11, verses 1–9. Why do you think they have been chosen?
2. In Advent we think of another coming of Jesus, besides his coming to Bethlehem. This coming is mentioned in the Apostles' Creed. Can you find and write out the words? It is also mentioned in the Advent hymn, 'Hark a thrilling voice is sounding'. Write out the first verse of this hymn and also the verse in which this other coming is mentioned.
3. Learn the Collect for the first Sunday in Advent.
4. Make an Advent ring. Here is a picture of one complete. Add one candle each Sunday during Advent. There are many ways of making an Advent ring. Ask a grown-up to help you.

17 *CHRISTMAS*

Christmas is a happy season, and especially for boys and girls, because they wonder what exciting new gift they are going to get. It is a time when we gather together as families in our homes; when we put up the Christmas decorations, sit down to our Christmas dinner, have parties and exchange presents.

But Christmas is also a great Church festival—the first in the year. You will remember that it was the first 'high place' on John's chart. At this season we prepare to celebrate the birthday of our Lord Jesus Christ (sometimes called *The Incarnation*) and the day chosen for his birthday is 25th December.

On Christmas Eve in our church we exchange the dark colours of Advent for the white of Christmas. It is all bright and gay with flowers and berries and evergreens. The Christmas crib is put in its place. There are extra services and special hymns and carols, in which we praise God as the angels did on the night our Saviour was born.

That night, as I expect you remember, some shepherds were watching their sheep on the hillsides of Bethlehem when an angel appeared to them and said, 'I have good news for you: there is great joy coming to the whole people. Today in the city of David a deliverer has been born to you—the Messiah, the Lord. And this is your sign: you will find a baby all wrapped up, in a manger.' And at once the shepherds heard a great chorus of angels singing, 'Glory to God in the highest,

and on earth peace, goodwill towards men.' The
shepherds went and found the infant Saviour in the
stable as the angel had said, and they worshipped him
there. You can see them doing this in the picture of the
Christmas Crib.

Ever since that day, Christian people have wanted to
give glory to God, and that is why the best and jolliest
hymns and carols belong to Christmas. Here is the story
of one of them. It is also the story of a Christmas present.
Just over two hundred years ago there lived at Kersall
in Lancashire a doctor called John Byrom. He had a

daughter called Dorothy, who was known by the family as Dolly. One year, not long before Christmas, Dr Byrom told Dolly that he would write her something special for Christmas Day and give it to her on Christmas morning. As 25th December drew nearer, Dolly grew more and more excited, wondering what this present could be. When she came down on Christmas morning there on her plate was an envelope addressed to her in her father's writing. She opened it and found some verses which started with the words:

> 'Christians awake! salute the happy morn
> Whereon the Saviour of mankind was born'.

But that is not the end of the story. The next Christmas Eve the doctor got a surprise as well as Dolly. The choir from the parish church came to the doctor's house and sang Dolly's carol, 'Christians awake', to a tune which the church organist, John Wainwright, had just written for it. It is the same tune that we sing to this Christmas carol today. You can see the choir, Dr Byrom and Dolly in the picture opposite.

So for more than two hundred years Dolly's Christmas present has given joy to countless people, and helped them to give glory to God in the Lord's house on the Lord's birthday. For it is in our church that our worship and praise is best offered on Christmas Day— whether it is Dolly's hymn we sing or some other. If our church had a voice, I think that it would say to young and old on Christmas Day,

> 'O come, let us adore him,
> Christ the Lord'.

Things to do

1. Make your own Christmas crib. You may have to ask a grown-up to help you. A crib can be made from quite simple materials.
2. Write these two lines underneath those about Advent in your note book:

    'While CHRISTMAS tells that he has come,
    A Babe in Bethlehem's lowly home.'

3. Make a list of your favourite carols and sing some of them at home during the holidays.

Harder things to do

1. Read the first four verses of 'Christians awake!' You will find them in your hymnbook. Look up the hard words in the dictionary or get a grown-up to help you. Now read in your Bible St Luke, chapter 2, verses 8–18 and find which Bible verses correspond to the verses of the hymn.
2. Find out and write down the meaning of INCARNATION. You may have to ask a grown-up to help you.
3. Read and think about a poem by Rudyard Kipling called *Eddi's Service*. (You may be able to borrow a copy of it at school.) Who really 'kept Christmas?' And why?

18 *EPIPHANY*

The feast of the Epiphany falls on 6th January. We keep it along with Christmas as a high festival in our church. John rightly put it in a high place on his chart. But the Epiphany is not as well remembered as it ought to be, perhaps because it is so near Christmas, and perhaps because it so often falls on a weekday that is not a holiday.

On the festival of the Epiphany we remember how wise men from the East came and worshipped Jesus, after following his star from their own land; and how they gave him gifts of gold, frankincense and myrrh. If you do not know the story well, you should find and read it now in your Bible. The story is in St Matthew's gospel, chapter 2, verses 1 to 12.

The word 'Epiphany' means *showing*, that is, the showing of Christ to the wise men. We know this from the second name for this festival in the Prayer Book. It is 'The Manifestation of Christ to the Gentiles.' Manifestation means 'showing' and 'Gentiles' means 'all people who are not Jews.' The wise men were the first people who were not Jews to come to the Lord Jesus.

Now let us think about the story, because it has something to say to us about *our* worship in *our* church. It all began, you remember, in a country far away from Palestine. There some wise men discovered a new star. This meant, according to their books, that a great king had been born. Imagine how excited they would be.

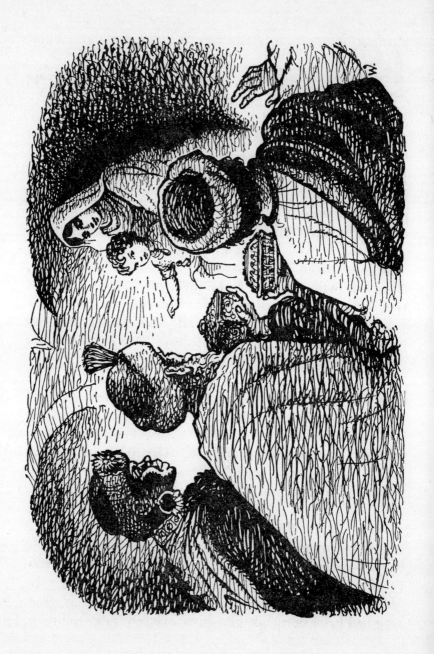

Perhaps one said, 'I would like to go and see this king, and offer him my gifts and my devotion.' 'So would I,' said another. 'Me too', said a third. So they *all decided to go together*.

That is the first thing the story says to us about *our* worship in *our* church. We should *all do it together*. You may sometimes go into church and find people kneeling quietly saying their prayers, and you may do this too whenever you want to, but our great acts of worship are when the family of God are gathered *all together*.

When the wise men set off, they found that God's star was showing them the way. It was a long, hard and dangerous journey through strange lands, across mountains, desert, seas and rivers. But *they wouldn't let anything stop them*. That is the second thing the story says to us about ourselves and our church. If we really want to worship the Lord Jesus, *we will not easily be stopped*. Difficulties are made to be overcome.

When at last the wise men arrived at the house in Bethlehem and found the Christ Child, *they offered him gifts* of gold, frankincense and myrrh. In the worship in our church *we too make gifts*, not only of our money but of ourselves.

> 'What can I give him
> Poor as I am?
> If I were a shepherd
> I would bring a lamb;
> If I were a wise man
> I would do my part;
> Yet what I can I give him—
> Give my heart.'

Things to do

1. Draw a picture of the wise men making their gifts to Jesus in the house at Bethlehem.
2. Write these two lines underneath those about Christmas in your notebook:

    'Then in the glad EPIPHANY
    To worship him come Wise Men three'.

3. Find out about the colours used in your church for (1) the Epiphany itself; (2) the season of Epiphany.
4. Write out the verse you like best in your favourite Epiphany hymn.

Harder things to do

1. Make a list of the things which prevent people from joining in public worship in church. If you can, put a tick against those which you think good reasons, and a cross against those you think to be only excuses.
2. Christ is being 'shown to the Gentiles' today wherever the Church is at work. See what you can find out about one special piece of Church work overseas, and collect pictures about the country concerned. You may be able to get help from missionary magazines.
3. Find out what the Collect for the Epiphany means and learn it by heart to use in your own prayers.
4. There are six Sundays after the Epiphany but they are not all wanted every year. Can you find out why?

19

LENT

The season of Lent begins in our Church on Ash Wednesday and ends on Good Friday and Easter Eve. It is a season of forty days, the same number of days that our Lord fasted in the wilderness. But if you count up from Ash Wednesday to Easter you will find there are forty-six days. The reason for this is that the six Sundays are not counted as part of Lent itself; they are called Sundays *in* Lent, not Sundays *of* Lent.

Lent is a 'getting ready' season to prepare us for Easter, but it is also more than this. It is a 'growing time'. The word 'lent' is an old English word for 'the spring'; but we do not chiefly think in Lent about the plants and flowers which grow and come out in the spring. We think rather about how we ourselves grow— in mind and soul as well as in body.

Have you a garden at home? If so, you may have heard something like this: 'I must clear away all the rubbish round that bush, and then cut out all the dead wood. It cannot possibly grow as it is.' Perhaps you have helped to do a job like that.

The season of Lent is a sort of 'cleaning up' time in our lives—a time to cut out anything that is bad or rotten, so that we can better grow into the sort of people God wants us to be. This we remember on the first day of Lent, which our Church calls Ash Wednesday. On that day in olden times people had ashes strewn on their heads as a sign that they were sorry for all that

was bad or evil in their lives. We do not use ashes so much this way nowadays, but we still begin Lent by confessing our wrong-doing and by trying to get rid of all that is bad and evil in our lives. In that way we may have a better chance to grow.

Now notice what the girl in the picture is doing. Her bulbs have flowered well because they have been watered regularly. All plants need water and the right food from the soil if they are to grow well.

We also need the right food and refreshment for our souls if we are to grow into the sort of people God wants us to be. Every Lent our Church helps us to remember this. There are extra services. We are invited to spend extra time on our prayers and our Bible-reading. And we are also invited to give up and do without something we like, during Lent, as a discipline for ourselves and to help us to do a little more for some part of God's work.

Things to do

1. Copy these two lines underneath those about Ephiphany into your notebook:

    'All through the forty days of LENT
    We try to grow—for sins repent.'

2. Notice any changes that are made in your church during Lent. What colour is used and why?
3. Attend any services or meetings specially arranged for boys and girls during Lent.

Harder things to do

1. Find in your Bible St Matthew, chapter 6, verses 16–18, and read there what Jesus taught his disciples about *fasting*. (Fasting means 'doing without food.')
2. Say an extra prayer during Lent. Here is one you might use. The words are from the Baptism service. 'Grant, O Lord, that I may never be ashamed to confess the faith of Christ crucified, and manfully to fight under his banner against sin, the world and the devil, and to continue Christ's faithful soldier and servant unto my life's end. Amen.'
3. Decide what you will give up during Lent, and to what part of God's work you will give extra help. There will probably be a Lent box, purse or envelope in church for you to have at home.

20 *GOOD FRIDAY*

The week before Easter which begins on Palm Sunday is called Holy Week. It is the most solemn time in our churches in all the Christian year. The story of Holy Week is told in all the four gospels and is read right through at Holy Communion during the week.

All through his life the Lord Jesus went about doing good. He *loved* people, and tried to help them, but there were some who *hated* Jesus for this and plotted against him. But he still went on loving and helping everyone, and he hoped that those who hated him would one day give up their hate and become his friends. Now let us think of what happened day by day during Holy Week.

Sunday. On this day, which we call Palm Sunday, Jesus rode into Jerusalem on a donkey. The disciples spread out their clothes and the children scattered palm branches on the road in front of him. They treated Jesus like a king, and all shouted in praise of God.

'Hosanna' they cried, 'blessed is he that cometh in the name of the Lord; hosanna in the highest.'

The jealous enemies of Jesus said to him, 'Stop them doing this', but he who loved his disciples and friends would not stop them from showing their love for him.

Monday and Tuesday. Jesus spent these two days teaching. He knew there were many who hated him.

His chief enemies tried to stop him from teaching by asking questions which they thought he couldn't answer; but they failed and Jesus went on teaching. Each night he went out to Bethany to stay with his friends there.

Wednesday. The priests met together and said, 'We must stop him; he must be put to death.'

While they were wondering how they could kill him, in came Judas Iscariot and said, 'If you give me money I will betray him to you.' They said 'We will give you thirty pieces of silver for betraying him.' How pleased they must have been! Judas had played into their hands. Now it would be easy to get rid of Jesus.

Thursday. On this day, often called Maundy Thursday in our Church, Judas betrayed Jesus into the hands of his enemies. It was after the Last Supper, when Jesus had gone with his disciples to the garden of Gethsemane. His enemies laughed at him and mocked him, but he said no unkind or complaining words.

Friday. On this day, which we now call Good Friday, the men who hated Jesus cried 'Crucify him'. He was being tried before Pontius Pilate. They got their way and Pontius Pilate ordered Jesus to be crucified. But even on the cross he still thought of his enemies: 'Father forgive them, for they know not what they do.' At three o'clock in the afternoon he died. His enemies seemed to have won; hate seemed to have beaten love. But it hadn't really. On Easter Day God raised Jesus from the dead. He rose again so that he might go on loving and helping all who try to follow him.

Things to do

1. Copy these lines into your notebook underneath those about Lent:

    'Through HOLY WEEK in thought and will
    We follow Christ to Calvary's hill.
    GOOD FRIDAY teaches of the Cross;
    Christ suffered to redeem our loss.'

2. Attend Holy Week services; or any holiday courses arranged for boys and girls.
3. Use the picture on the opposite page in your prayers each day and say

    'O dearly, dearly has he loved,
    And we must love him too,
    And trust in his redeeming Blood,
    And try his works to do.'

Harder things to do

1. Give the reasons why these days in Holy Week have special names in our Church: *Palm* Sunday, *Maundy* Thursday, *Good* Friday.
2. Read the story of Holy Week right through as it is told in St Mark's gospel, chapters 11–15. Use J. B. Phillips's translation or *The New English Bible* for this if you can.
3. Prepare the Easter garden, if you are going to make one.
4. Learn the first Collect for Good Friday.

21

EASTER

Easter is the queen of all the Church festivals. On Easter Day we remember that Jesus Christ rose from the dead. Here is part of that wonderful story.

On the Friday evening the friends of Jesus took down his body from the cross and carried it away to the garden of Joseph of Arimathea. There Joseph wrapped it in linen and they laid it in a tomb hewn out of the solid rock. They rolled a great stone in front of the opening and went away. The next day was the sabbath, the Jews' day of rest. It must have been a very sad day for the disciples. No doubt they thought they would never see Jesus again.

Then came the first day of the Jews' week, the day we call Sunday. Mary Magdalene set out for the tomb in Joseph's garden very early. It was still quite dark. When she got there, she found the stone rolled away. Even then she did not guess what had happened. 'Someone has been here and stolen his body', she thought. So she ran through the silent streets to tell the other disciples. 'They have taken the Lord out of the tomb', she said, 'and I don't know where they have laid him.'

Peter and John went back with Mary. When they got to the tomb, Peter went inside and made sure the tomb was empty. In the picture you can see him saying so to Mary and John. After Peter and John had left, Mary stayed in the garden. She was crying. She turned and found someone standing there. It was Jesus himself, but

she thought he was the gardener.

'Oh sir', she said, 'if you have carried him away,
please tell me where you have put him.'

Then Jesus spoke her name. 'Mary', he said.

She turned excitedly and cried, 'Master!'

Jesus said to her. 'Go back and tell the other disciples
that you have seen me.'

How happy Mary must have been! At last she knew
that Jesus had come back again. He had risen from the
dead. He was alive for evermore.

Later that day Jesus appeared to other disciples,
including two who were going from Jerusalem to
Emmaus, a village about five miles away. As they walked,
Jesus joined them and went with them along the road,
but they didn't know who he was. When they got to
Emmaus it was nearly dark, and the disciples invited

their companion to stay the night with them. During the evening meal, Jesus broke the bread just as he had done at the Last Supper and often before that. Then, suddenly, the disciples knew who he was! At last they had recognized their Master as we can see in the picture on this page. They rushed back to Jerusalem to tell the others that they had seen the Lord. When they got there they found that the other disciples knew already that Jesus had risen from the dead. 'The Lord is risen indeed', they said, 'and has appeared to Peter.'

This wonderful news makes Easter the happiest day in all the year. This is why our church is gay with lilies and other flowers. This is why we have done away with all the dark colours of Lent, and why we sing our joyful Easter hymns with their ringing alleluias.

Things to do

1. Copy these lines into your notebook underneath those about Good Friday:

    'At EASTER Christ, who died to save,
    In triumph rises from the grave.'

2. Make and decorate an Easter card, using the words: 'The Lord is risen. Alleluia.'
3. Write out a verse of your favourite Easter hymn.

Harder things to do

1. Read St John, chapter 20; St Luke, chapter 24; and 1 Corinthians, chapter 15, verses 3–8, if possible from J. B. Phillips's translation or *The New English Bible*. (This should be spread over several days.)
2. Set up the Easter garden.
3. A new church decides to have a stained glass window at the east end, over the altar. There are three panels. The church council want it to be an 'Easter window.' Say what you think it should contain, and, if you can, design and paint it also.
4. Read the words of the Easter anthems from *The New English Bible* and learn the Easter Day Collect. (The Easter anthems are in the Prayer Book just before the Collect for Easter Day.)

22 *THE ASCENSION*

Ascension Day comes exactly forty days after Easter Day in the calendar of our Church. There were forty days also between the first Easter Day and the first Ascension Day. During those forty days the Lord Jesus often appeared to his apostles and talked to them about the work they were to do. He said, 'You are to go and make disciples of all the nations, and baptize them in the name of the Father, and of the Son, and of the Holy Spirit. Teach them to observe all that I have commanded you, and remember, I am with you always, even to the end of the world.'

When the Ascension Day came, Jesus was with his disciples as they were gathered together in Jerusalem. There he had another message for them. He told them not to leave Jerusalem. He said, 'You must wait till my Father has fulfilled the promise that he made. I have often spoken to you about it. John, as you know, baptized with water, but you will be baptized with the Holy Spirit, and within the next few days. That is how my Father will fulfil his promise.'

Then the Lord Jesus led his friends out of Jerusalem along the Bethany Road, and on to the Mount of Olives. It was a road they knew well. They had come along this same road only a few weeks before, when the Lord Jesus entered Jerusalem riding on a donkey, and the grown-ups and children shouted 'Hosanna'.

Presently they reached the top of the hill just above

Bethany. There Jesus spoke his last words to his friends. 'You are to be witnesses to me, not only in Jerusalem, not only throughout Judea, not only in Samaria, but to the very ends of the earth.'

When he had said this, he was lifted up before their eyes till a cloud hid him from their sight. So he 'ascended into heaven', to sit 'on the right hand of God the Father Almighty.' Jesus returned home to his heavenly Father, and all the angels of God welcomed him with lovely songs of praise and joy.

But in all that joy and glory, Jesus did not forget his friends below. He sent two angels to speak to them.

'Men of Galilee', they said, 'why are you standing here looking up into the sky? This very Jesus who has been taken up from you into heaven will come back in just the same way as you have seen him go.'

Jesus knew that message would comfort them. He knew they would go back to Jerusalem to wait for the Holy Spirit to come and give them power.

Turn back to page 85 and look at John's chart of the Christian Year. You will see that John made Ascension Day one of the 'high places', for it is one of the five great feasts of the Church.

In places where there are 'church schools', Ascension Day is a very special day. Boys and girls assemble as on other days, but not for usual school work. Instead they go to the parish church for a service of praise and thanksgiving for the ascension of Jesus to his Father in heaven. The rest of the day is a holiday and sometimes there are games and sports. In that way the boys and girls join with other members of God's family in keeping the festival.

Things to do

1. Add these lines to your notebook underneath those about Easter:

   'Then follow the GREAT FORTY DAYS
   Kept by the Church with joy and praise.
   ASCENSION tells, Christ glorified,
   Returns to God the Father's side.'

2. Letter and illuminate 'He ascended into heaven,' (Apostles' Creed).
3. Try and find photographs and pictures of the Mount of Olives as it is today, and paste them in your scrap album. You may be able to borrow some transparencies and show them to your friends.
4. Write out and learn the verse you like best in your favourite Ascension-tide hymn.

Harder things to do

1. Find and read the story of the ascension in Acts, chapter 1, verses 1–14. Use a modern translation if you can.
2. Write out and learn the Collect for Ascension Day; or write a new hymn (or even a verse of one) for use on Ascension Day.
3. Psalm 24 is sung on Ascension Day. Say if you think it is a good choice and why.

23 *WHITSUNDAY*

Whitsunday is the festival of God the Holy Spirit and is the fourth of the five chief festivals of the Christian Year. You may like to know how it came to have this name. In olden times it was the custom for large numbers of people to come to their parish church together for baptism on this day. They all wore white and so the Sunday came to be known as 'White Sunday', or 'Whitsunday' as we say today.

The story of Whitsunday is the story of the birthday of the Church. This is what happened. After Jesus had ascended into heaven, the apostles went back to Jerusalem, to the upstairs room they knew so well. You will remember from the last chapter how Jesus had told them to wait until they received God's promised gift. No doubt during the days of waiting they thought and talked and prayed about the great work they were to do for the Lord Jesus.

Meanwhile every day more and more people came streaming into Jerusalem. They had come to keep the feast of Pentecost, which was their harvest festival. There were Jews from near and far. Every house was full; there were even tents pitched on the hills around.

At last the great day came. While the Jews were keeping the feast of Pentecost in the temple, wonderful things were happening in the upper room. Suddenly there came from the sky a noise like that of a strong, driving wind. It filled the whole house where they

were sitting. There appeared among them tongues like flames of fire, resting on each one. God's promised gift had come at last. You can see a picture of this on this page. The apostles were filled with the power of the Holy Spirit; they felt strong and brave, and ready for the work Jesus had called them to do.

Soon they were out in the crowded streets, boldly preaching Jesus. Peter was the chief speaker. He said to the people, 'You have made an awful mistake; the Jesus whom you crucified is risen from the dead. Repent, before it is too late. Be baptized and become his disciples.'

That day three thousand people came forward to join up with the apostles. So the good news was spread on the first Whitsunday, and so the Church started. All through the centuries the work of telling the good news

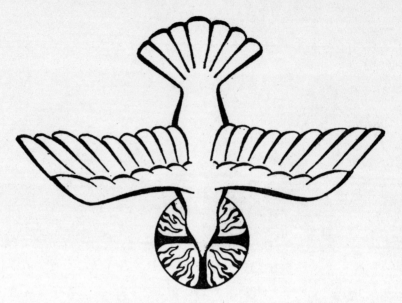

about Jesus Christ has gone on. It is still going on in our Church today.

Sometimes in church you will see the figure of a dove flying downwards, like that on this page. It stands for God the Holy Spirit who came like a dove upon our Lord when he was baptized by John the Baptist in the River Jordan. Whenever we see the picture of the dove flying downwards, it helps us to remember the Holy Spirit. He has come down from God to be our Guide and Teacher. He is our Friend from heaven above, as he was to the apostles long ago.

To him the Church prays not only on Whitsunday, but at other times too:

'Come, gracious Spirit, heavenly Dove,
With light and comfort from above;
Be thou our guardian, thou our guide,
O'er every thought and step preside.'

Things to do

1. Add these lines to your notebook underneath those for Ascension Day:

    'At WHITSUN God the Spirit came
    As mighty wind, as living flame.'

2. What colour is used in your church on Whitsunday and why?
3. Use this prayer each day during Whitsun week:

    'Holy Spirit hear us,
    Friend from heaven above;
    Thou art ever near us,
    Fill our hearts with love.'

4. Draw a picture of Peter preaching to the people on the first Whitsunday.

Harder things to do

1. Read the story of Whitsunday in Acts, chapter 2. This should be spread over several days. Use a modern translation if you can. Find on the map the countries and places mentioned in verses 8–11. Who would have the longest journey to Jerusalem? How would they travel?
2. Learn and use the Collect for Whitsunday. If you are not sure what it means, ask an adult to help you.
3. Three things we know are used to describe God the Holy Ghost. What are we meant to learn about him when we say he is (1) like wind; (2) like fire; (3) like a dove?

24 *TRINITY SUNDAY*

Trinity Sunday is the last of the five great festivals of the Christian year. After it has passed there are 'Sundays after Trinity' for nearly six months. Then we come round again to Advent and the beginning of yet another Church year.

You may like to know what the word 'Trinity' means. It means 'three-in-one.' On Trinity Sunday we try to think about how wonderful God is. There are three ways specially in which we can think about God. Sometimes we think of the heavenly Father, who made us all and cares for us all. Sometimes we think of the Lord Jesus Christ, his Son. Sometimes we think of the Holy Spirit, whom he sent to help his disciples and to be with us all since he ascended into heaven. And in a wonderful way which we do not understand, and no one understands, when we think about the Father, or the Son, or the Holy Spirit, we are thinking about God.

There is a story told of Patrick, who first took the good news about the Lord Jesus Christ to the Irish. One day some Irish chieftains came to him and said, 'You speak to us of God the Father, God the Son, and God the Holy Ghost—yet only one God. How can this be?'

Patrick replied by picking up a shamrock leaf. He showed them its three parts. 'You see that this leaf is in three parts', he said, 'yet it is only one leaf. It is made three in one. That is how I think about God.'

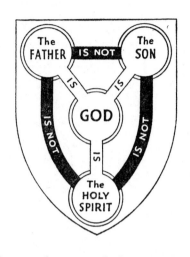

You can see Patrick using the shamrock leaf for his teaching in the picture at the foot of this page.

In olden days a shield, like that on the left, was often put up where people could see it. It shows in another way what Patrick tried to teach through the shamrock.

On Trinity Sunday we try to think of all that we know about God, but we do so in order to give him glory and worship. One of God's servants long ago, who thought much about him, had a wonderful vision or dream in which he saw God's glory. Afterwards he tried

to write it down. The words that he wrote are always read as the epistle on Trinity Sunday. Here are some of the worship parts that come in it.

'Holy, holy, holy is God the sovereign Lord
    of all, who was, and is, and is to come!'
'Thou art worthy, O Lord our God, to
    receive glory and honour and power,
    because thou didst create all things; by thy
    will they were created, and have their
    being.'

To these words we may add others often used in our Church, and with them we will end our book.

'Glory be to the Father, and to the Son: and to
    the Holy Ghost;
As it was in the beginning, is now, and ever
    shall be: world without end. Amen.'

Things to do

1. Add these lines in your notebook underneath those for Whitsunday:

   > 'At TRINITY we worship thee
   > One living God in Persons three.'

   Now that you have lines describing the whole Church year, you may like to learn them by heart.
2. Find out about the colours in your church, used (1) on Trinity Sunday, (2) in the Trinity season.
3. Find in your hymnbook the hymn 'Holy, holy, holy, Lord God Almighty'. Write out and learn the last verse.

Harder things to do

1. Read the whole of the epistle for Trinity Sunday, if possible in a modern translation. You may want to talk about it to a grown-up.
2. Opposite is a design you may see sometimes in a church. A fish stands for a Christian. Three fish arranged roughly in the form of a triangle are to show that Christians are baptized in the name of the Trinity—Father, Son, and Holy Ghost. Make a fair copy of the design and say, if you can, *why* the fish is the symbol of the Christian, and *why* the triangle is the symbol of the Trinity.
3. See if you can find out how Trinidad got its name.